Exotic
TURKEY

Dr. Diana Prince

AuthorHouse™
1663 Liberty Drive
Bloomington, IN 47403
www.authorhouse.com
Phone: 833-262-8899

Because of the dynamic nature of the Internet, any web addresses or links contained in this book may have changed
since publication and may no longer be valid. The views expressed in this work are solely those of the author and do not
necessarily reflect the views of the publisher, and the publisher hereby disclaims any responsibility for them.

All photographs in this book are the sole property of the author.

This book is printed on acid-free paper.

ISBN: 979-8-8230-2594-2 (sc)
ISBN: 979-8-8230-2596-6 (hc)
ISBN: 979-8-8230-2595-9 (e)

Library of Congress Control Number: 2024908575

Print information available on the last page.

Published by AuthorHouse 05/17/2024

authorHOUSE®

Contents

Introduction

The book, *Exotic Turkey*, explores this ancient country and its people. Over one hundred full color photos introduce the reader to Turkey's remarkable beauty and treasures.

After centuries, the ancient city of Istanbul still retains its mystique. From its mosques to its museums, it captures the wonder of this place. Turkey combines its remarkable beauty with its rich history.

In Cappadocia, explore its ancient underground cities. In Ephesus, witness some of mankind's most remarkable architecture, from its ancient temples to the world's largest amphitheater.

Join pilgrims at the site of a thousand-year old church on Akdamar Island. Outside of Ephesus, visit the 2,000 year old house of the Virgin Mary. She had been brought here by St. John the Apostle after the death of Christ.

Enjoy the ancient treasures in the country's unforgettable museums.

And in a special included feature, explore first-hand the remarkable site of Noah's Ark near the ancient village of Dogubayazit.

Turkey is unforgettable. It captures both the mind and the heart.

Istanbul Mosque

Chapter One

Istanbul

Istanbul is located on the Bosporus, in effect becoming a bridge between Europe and Asia. In ancient times, Istanbul was known by several names. Originally it was the ancient Greek city of Halicarnassus. In the Sixth Century BC, it was known as Byzantium. By the Third Century AD, it was known as Constantinople.

Astoundingly, Istanbul has been the capital of four major empires. The first was the Roman Empire in 300 AD. The second was the Byzantine Empire in the Fourth through the Twelfth Century AD. The third was the Latin Empire in the Twelfth Century AD. It was also the capital of the Ottoman Empire in the 15th Century through 1922.

One of the most astounding sights in Istanbul is the massive Basilica Cistern located under the city. It dates to the Byzantine Era. Designed in the year 532 AD, it originally supplied water to the Great Palace. Over three hundred massive columns support the roof of the Cistern. Each pillar is almost 30 feet high. An extensive labyrinth of walkways extend over the water underneath, creating an unusual and cavernous view. Above the walkways there are several large stone pillars supporting the massive structure. The shadows and underground lighting give it the otherworldly effect of a massive underground cathedral.

Nearby, the Blue Mosque, built in 1609 is still an active mosque today. There are 13 domes, and six soaring minarets, which grace the skyline with their graceful spires. At night, a flood of blue lights illuminates the Mosque.

In the Kadikoy District, visitors gather to buy fresh produce and Turkish specialties, which include the popular flat bread called "gosleme". One of the city's greatest tourist destinations is Istanbul's "Grand Bazaar". It is a massive, stunning indoor market with elaborate archways and about 3,000 separate shops. It covers the equivalent of 60 streets within its labyrinth of massive archways. It is easy to get lost in the passageways of shops and businesses.

Nearby, the Topkapi Palace dates to the 15th Century. It is located in the Karakoy district of Istanbul. It was home to the Ottoman sultans for four centuries.

Also, in the Karakoy district is the Elegant Hagia Sophia. For 1,000 years it was a Christian

Church. In 1453, when the Ottomans conquered Constantinople, it became a mosque. It was briefly a museum in 1934, but today it is again a mosque.

A frequent destination near Istanbul is to the nearby town of Bodrum. It is an ancient town with spectacular Bodrum Castle overlooking the Aegean Sea. It is one of the premier tourist destinations. It was built in the 1400's by the Knights of St. John. The inviting sandy beaches, thriving culture and busy night life make Istanbul a thriving destination for tourists.

Bodrum Castle

Topkapi Palace

Shop in Istanbul

Craftsman at Work in Istanbul

6

Morning in Istanbul

7

Alleyway in Istanbul

Shopping for Rugs

Shop Owner

Chickens for Sale

Shopping in Istanbul Indoor Bazaar

Winding Alleyway

Colorful Spice Market

14

Family Restaurant in Istanbul

Looking for Shopping Treasures

Fruit Vendor

17

Afternoon Break

Courtyard of Mosque in Istanbul

Elaborate Art Work on Display

Park Near Mosque in Istanbul

Restaurant in the Park

Istanbul Waterfront

Kadikoy Iskelesi Ferry Terminal in Istanbul

Inside Ancient Christian Church in Istanbul

Sunset in Istanbul

Ancient Stela in Istanbul Museum

27

Chapter Two

Museum Treasures

Ephesus Museum

One of the finest museums in Turkey is the *Ephesus Archaeological Museum* in Selcuk. Many of the exhibits are from the excavation site in the vicinity of ancient Ephesus. One of the most important finds exhibited in the Ephesus Museum is the statue of the Goddess "Artemis", also known as "Diana" to the Romans.

The temple to the goddess "Artemis" stood in what was once the most sacred and important site in the ancient world. Centuries of time have taken their toll. Little is left of that great site which has witnessed the passing of the centuries.

Istanbul Archaeological Museums

The Istanbul Archaeological Museum has three separate archaeological collections, located in the vicinity of the Topkapi Palace in Istanbul. They house a comprehensive collection of objects. Most are displayed to emphasize the different periods of Turkey's history. These include early pre historic items, as well as several amazing finds from subsequent centuries.

The largest complex of the Istanbul Archaeological Museum is divided into three comprehensive collections which fill three massive buildings.

The Istanbul Archaeological Museum was built by Sultan Abdulaziz who opened the extensive collections to the public in the Nineteenth Century.

The Istanbul Archeological Museum documents the treasures of the Ottoman Empire up to the period of the Imperial Museum in the 1800's.

The treasures on display date to the Egyptian, Greek and Arabian periods. They also extensively document important archaeological finds from the Ottoman Empire.

Museum Walkway with Artifacts

Ancient History Written in Stone

Ancient Weapons on Display in Museum Exhibit

Elaborate Islamic Art

ان الصلوة على المؤمنين كتابا موقوتا

32

Homes Among the Rocks

Chapter Three

The Underground City at Cappadocia

Cappadocia is located in the region called the Anatolia Plain. The region has an unusual and otherworldly landscape. Because it was an ancient volcanic area, it produced a landscape of soft volcanic rock. The porous rock was covered by a layer of basalt. This substance called "tufa" covers the landscape for miles. Wind and rain over thousands of years have created pinnacles and cones, which locals today refer to as "fairy chimneys."

The region of Cappadocia has been estimated to have possibly thirty underground cities. Only a few of these have been explored and excavated. In those few cities which have been found and explored, underground finds included ancient cisterns and rooms among the ancient passageways.

These underground homes built into the rock provided giant air shafts to ventilate the underground rooms. These findings provided evidence of sophisticated solutions by the ancient builders who created them.

The soft rock, which was carved out over time with underground rooms and passageways, has remained an enigma. These rooms and tunnels testify to ancient man's abilities to accommodate and adapt to his environment. There are even remains of underground "churches" in this maze of tunnels and underground construction.

The region of Goreme in the Botan Canyon of Cappadocia is one of the areas where the "fairy chimney" is commonly seen. Each one is the unexpected result of a geological process that began millions of years ago, when volcanic eruptions rained ash over this region of Turkey. Subsequently, the rain and wind carved the unusual landscape we find here today.

What looks today like a village that might have been built by elves was, in fact, a complex of engineered underground construction.

Near this region, in the city called Perge, Saint Paul preached here in the year 40 AD. At that time, this region also had large Roman baths constructed among the rocks. There is even evidence of a large stone marketplace which was built here at that time.

Cappadocia Dwellings

Vista of Fairy Chimenys

An Entry Way to Underground Rooms

Large Underground Complex

Doorway to Underground Complex

Aerial View of Cappadocia

Fairy Chimneys among the Hills

View from the Summit of Cappadocia

Exploring Underground Tunnels

Finding Underground Rooms

44

Vista of Underground Homes

Underground Church

Village of "Fairy Chimneys"

Tower Lookout

The Ancient City of Ephesus

Chapter Four

Ancient City Of Ephesus

The ancient town of Ephesus lies in the beautiful region of Anatolia. The ancient city has been significant since ancient times. It is located in Ismir Province near the towns of Selcuk and Kusadasi.

One of the most visited and significant Roman buildings in Ephesus is the magnificent Library of Celsus. The walls, though preserved in time, are in disrepair after the passage of centuries. Yet, the architectural grace and flawless design attest to its former splendor. The ancient library in Ephesus dates to the year 117 AD. The Library at Celsus, beautiful in design, was also the repository of over 10,000 scrolls.

The significant architecture in the ancient city reflects the influence of the Greek, Roman and Christion Eras which flourished here. It was a magnificent city. In Ephesus, there is a grand theater which could hold over 20,000 spectators. It was built in 1000 BC, after the classical Greek Era. It was part of the Roman Republic in the first century BC. The wide streets and thoroughfares of the old city were created on a grand and monumental scale.

The Temple of Artemis, built in the sixth century BC by Croesus, took an estimated 120 years to complete. To the Romans, it was known as the Temple of Diana, who was the Roman version of the goddess by that name.

The Temple of Artemis is considered one of the "Seven Wonders of the World". The dimensions of that building would have made it twice the size of the Parthenon in Athens, Greece. The Greek poet, Antipater, in 200 BCE, called it the grandest of all buildings "surpassing Babylon and even the Great Pyramid." At that time, it was the largest building in the world. Today only remnants of the magnificent stone building remain.

Today a singular soaring pillar marks the place where that magnificent Temple of Artemis once stood. That pillar, which towers above the vast field of fallen stones, is all that remains of what was once the grandest and most sacred of the ancient sites. It was put together from the fragments of fallen stones from the Temple. It stands alone in the vast field which once had some of the most astounding architecture in the history of the world. Nearby, there are other sights for tourists. In Kusadasi, there is an Aqua Water Park. There are also boat tours along the Aegean coast with visits to Pigeon Island.

One of the finest museums in Turkey is the Ephesus Archaeological Museum in Selcuk. Many of the exhibits are from the excavation site in the vicinity of ancient Ephesus.

Camels Relaxing

The Ancient City of Ephesus

Colonnade near Ancient Theater

Tourists Visit Ancient Street in Ephesus

Temple of Diana at Ephesus showing a section of the last
remaining pillar from that Ancient Temple

Ancient City of Ephesus with modern buildings in the Distance

The last remaining column of the Temple of the Goddess Artemis reconstructed from some of the pieces of the original column after an earthquake.

Remains of the Ancient Theater in Ephesus

Tourists on the Ancient Streets of Ephesus

Street in Ephesus with a Small Temple

Ancient Room

Ancient Library of Celsius

Steps Leading to the House of the Virgin Mary in Ephesus

Chapter Five

House of the Virgin Mary

Ephesus is located close to the towns of Ismir and Selcuk. This is the place where Saint John the Apostle brought the Virgin Mary after the death of her son, Jesus. Here she spent the remainder of her life in his care. Her grave is believed to be in Ephesus, but others have claimed that it is in Jerusalem.

In the green hills and forested area of Selcuk, just outside of the city of Ephesus, is a modest stone building believed for millennia to have been the house where the Virgin Mary lived the final days of her life, after the crucifixion of her son. Tradition states that of the others who gathered in this place, only Mary's house was built of stone. Many believe that she was cared for here and guarded by the apostle John, who had taken her there to live in safety. Both Christians and Muslims make pilgrimages to this place which is believed to have been the final home of the Virgin Mary. Today, it is a destination of religious pilgrims from around the world who gather here to honor the mother of Christ. The home is maintained by both nuns and Catholic monks.

Mary Magdalen had also been brought to live in Ephesus by the Apostle John, according to tradition. She spent several years in a nearby cave in the mountains in repentance for her sins. Traditions say that she died there and was buried there, after spending many years in a cave in the mountain repenting for her sins.

Today pilgrims come from around the world to see where the mother of Jesus lived the last years of her life. The original stone steps still lead up to the house. The stone exterior is nestled in a grove of trees. Immediately upon entering the home, the stone fireplace is facing the door. It is here where the Virgin Mary is said to have lived the final years of her life, and she is believed to have died within this house.

In Turkish, the house of Mary is called "Meryemana Evi", which means "Mary's House". The house was built in the foothills of Mount Koressos on the outskirts of Ephesus. The site, itself, is located 7km from Selcuk. This location is also known as "Bulbul Mountain."

It is also believed that this was the place of Mary's Assumption into heaven upon her death.

The House of the Virgin Mary in Ephesus

Sign Pointing the Way to the House of the Virgin Mary

Altar inside the House of the Virgin Mary

Two Images of the Virgin Mary within the house

Local Villager

Chapter Six

People Of Turkey

Of all of the treasures in Turkey, one of the greatest is the people who live there. With a genuine friendliness and warmth, they are a collage of many interests.

Here artists, philosophers, machinists, teachers and travelers reflect their ancient past, and plan the future in their everyday lives.

They move into that future with vision, hard work and enthusiasm. They are an extraordinary people in an extraordinary country.

The photos in this chapter show their warmth, and demonstrate their zest for life.

Watermelons for Sale

Man with His Puppy

Observation Point on the Istanbul Shore

Two Young Girls in Dogubayazit

Observation Point on the Istanbul Shore

David Fasold Holding a Puppy

Woman Making a Rug

Choosing a Rug in Istanbul

Performers Doing Traditional Turkish Dance

Craftsman at Work in Pottery Shop

Shop Keeper in Turkish Crafts Shop

Games Arcade in Istanbul

Turkish Rugs for Sale

Chickens for Sale

Young Boy in Village

A Performing Bear

Craftsman at Work

On the Outskirts of Istanbul

Istanbul Harbor

Men Aboard Boat in Istanbul Harbor

Church on Akdamar Island

Chapter Seven

Ancient Church at Akdamar Island

Akdamar Island is the home of Lake Van, Turkey's largest lake. It is also home to the Armenian Holy Cross Cathedral. Built in the Tenth Century by the Armenians, it has flourished since 1116 AD. Today visitors can reach the Church by ferry boat. Akdamar Island has been popular since Medieval Times. It was originally called "The Church for Kings". The kings of Vaspurakan were the first to attend services here.

Inside the cavernous church are elaborate carvings depicting scenes from the Bible. The majority of adherents to the Holy Cross Cathedral identify with the Armenian Apostolic Church and its Eastern Christian rites.

Two specific groups comprise the adherents. The first is the "Armenian Apostolic" sect which has its origin in the rites of Oriental Orthodoxy. The second group is the Armenian Catholic sect.

Both Saint Bartholomew and Saint Jude Thaddeus came to this island in the year 300AD. They were the first to preach and convert this region. Ultimately both Bartholomew and St. Thaddeus were martyrs for their faith, executed by the Armenian king.

In the Armenian religion, the Biblical books are referred to as "the Breath of God" because they are believed to be the words of God Himself revealed to man.

Today the Armenian sect here worships Jesus, and has a great devotion to the Virgin Mary. It recognizes the validity of precepts in the Roman Catholic community, as well as in the Eastern rites.

Local legends say that angels go into and out of the water around Akdamar Island and they believe that the island itself is "enchanted". Legend also says that in 7000 BC, seven falling comets created this lake. However, others say it was caused by massive flooding in ancient times.

After centuries, the Church had fallen into disrepair. In 2007, the Turkish government repaired the structure and it became a museum open to the public.

Tourist Boat to Akdamar Island

Small Boat to Akdamar Island

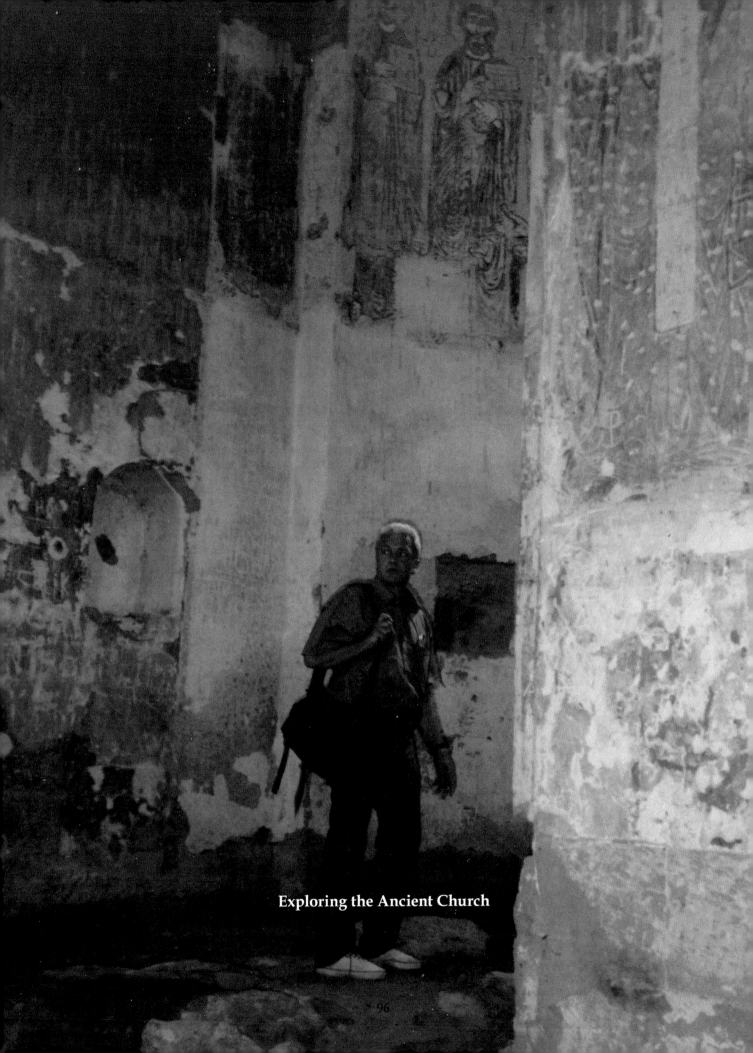

Exploring the Ancient Church

Main Window in Church Interior

Door in East Alcove of the Church on Akdamar Island

Turtle on the Ancient Stones of the Church on Akdamar Island

Anchor Stone from Noah's Ark (Vertical)

Chapter Eight

Noah's Ark Site in Dogubayazit

In 1948, a strong earthquake pushed a boat-shaped object up into a remote area in Turkey near Mount Ararat. The event generated great interest, and the area was later photographed from ten thousand feet by a Turkish reconnaissance plane. This remarkable photo appeared in the September 5, 1960 issue of Life Magazine.

The Bible had specified that the Ark had set down on the "Mountains of Ararat". Similarly, the Koran had mentioned a specific mountain called "Mount Judi". The Koran had also mentioned the "Great Flood". The ship in Turkey was located near the town of Dogubayazit in Turkey at an altitude of 6,300 feet. It came to be called the "Durupinar Site". A number of scientists came to investigate the boat-shaped site in Turkey.

One of these was David Fasold. an American researcher. He first came to the site in 1977. Using the "Royal Egyptian" cubit for measurement, the length of the ship was confirmed to be the equivalent of 515 feet. His measurements confirmed that the Turkish ship exactly matched the equivalent Biblical dimension with respect to length.

David Fasold had formerly been with the United States Merchant Marines and had traveled the world. He had spent years operating a successful salvaging business in Florida and exploring sunken ships and aircraft. He was a close friend of the legendary Mel Fisher.

As one of the leading investigators, Fasold spent nine years conducting scientific investigations at the Ark site. He brought his comprehensive nautical skills and understanding of fluid dynamics together with his knowledge of ancient cultures. He then used new technology to answer old questions.

Fasold used a molecular frequency generator, and later, ground-penetrating radar, which was a technology formerly used in NASA projects. But it was his keen ability to put the pieces together into a coherent whole that brought his work to the attention of the world.

Recognized by Turkey's High Commission for Noah's Ark, and under the direction of Dr. Salye Baraktutan of Ataturk University in Erzerum, Turkey, Fasold was the only non-Turkish person ever allowed to sit as a member of Turkey's "High Commission of Noah's Ark".

He collaborated with other key investigators. He worked with American adventurer Ron Wyatt, and with physicist Jon Baumgardner from Los Alamos Lab. He also worked with astronaut Colonel Irwin. As a former Marine Salvage operator, Fasold also did scanning with three types of metal detectors. Sub-surface radar scans revealed equidistantly placed bulk heads in the ship. Metallurgy studies identified them as "fossilized timber sealed with pitch".

Overview of the Ark Site

Turkish Soldiers Guarding the Ark Site

Crossing the River by Truck

Village Children Near the Ark Site

Cattle Graze near the Ark Site

David Fasold, Ark Researcher, sitting on Petrified Ballast from the Ark

Petrified Reed-Covered Ballast from the Ark

Author with One of the Anchor Stones

Village of Kazan with Mount Ararat in the Background

Local Village Children near the Art Site

Local Farmer near the Ark Site

Printed in the United States
by Baker & Taylor Publisher Services